Contents

Introduction:

Chapter 1

Understanding Digital Marketing

Chapter 2

Key Components of Digital Marketing

Chapter 3:

Developing a Digital Marketing Strategy

Chapter 4:

Creating Compelling Content

Chapter 5:

Maximizing Your Website's Potential

Chapter 6:

Harnessing the Power of Social Media

Chapter 7:

Email Marketing Essentials

Chapter 8:

Leveraging Paid Advertising

Chapter 9:

Measuring Success and Analytics

Conclusion

MASTERING DIGITAL MARKETING:
STRATEGIES FOR SUCCESS IN THE DIGITAL AGE

AUTHOR BOOK
ROSE JORDAN

Mastering Digital Marketing: Strategies for Success in the Digital Age

Introduction:

In a world where technology evolves at breakneck speed and consumer behavior undergoes constant transformation, traditional marketing strategies are rapidly becoming outdated. Welcome to the era of digital marketing, where innovation and connectivity reign supreme.

Gone are the days of relying solely on billboards, print ads, and cold calls to reach your audience. Today, businesses of all sizes must embrace the digital landscape to stay competitive and relevant. Whether you're a seasoned marketer looking to expand your skillset or an entrepreneur navigating the complexities of online promotion, this e-book is your roadmap to success in the digital age.

Join us on a journey through the dynamic realm of digital marketing, where creativity meets data-driven strategy to captivate audiences and drive business growth. From mastering the intricacies of SEO and social media to crafting compelling content and harnessing the power of email marketing, this comprehensive guide equips you with the tools and knowledge to thrive in today's ever-evolving digital ecosystem.

Prepare to unlock the secrets of effective digital marketing, discover innovative techniques to engage your target audience, and elevate your brand to new heights of success. Whether you're a newcomer to the world of digital marketing or a seasoned professional seeking fresh insights, this e-book is your ultimate companion on the path to digital marketing mastery.

Are you ready to revolutionize your marketing approach and propel your business forward in the digital era? Let's embark on this transformative journey together and unlock the limitless potential of digital marketing.

Welcome to the future of marketing. Welcome to the digital marketing revolution.

Chapter 1

Understanding Digital Marketing

- What is Digital Marketing?

In today's fast-paced and interconnected world, traditional marketing methDigital marketing encompasses a broad range of online tactics and strategies designed to connect businesses with their target audience through digital channels. Unlike traditional marketing, which primarily relies on offline mediums such as print ads, billboards, and television commercials, digital marketing leverages the power of the internet and electronic devices to deliver targeted messages to consumers wherever they are.

At its core, digital marketing is about building and nurturing relationships with customers in the online sphere. It involves understanding consumer behavior, identifying their needs and preferences, and delivering personalized experiences that resonate with them. From increasing brand awareness and driving website traffic to generating leads and boosting sales, digital marketing offers a myriad of opportunities for businesses to achieve their marketing objectives effectively and efficiently.

Chapter 2

Key Components of Digital Marketing

- **Website Optimization**

Website optimization involves fine-tuning various elements of your site to improve its functionality, speed, and relevance to both users and search engines. By optimizing your website, you can enhance user satisfaction, increase engagement, and ultimately drive conversions and sales.

Key Components of Website Optimization:

1. Speed Optimization: In today's fast-paced world, users expect websites to load quickly. Slow-loading pages can lead to high bounce rates and decreased conversions. Speed optimization techniques include optimizing images, leveraging browser caching, and minimizing HTTP requests to improve load times.

2. Mobile Responsiveness: With the increasing use of mobile devices, it's essential to ensure that your website is optimized for mobile users. A responsive design adapts seamlessly to various screen sizes and devices, providing a consistent and user-friendly experience across desktops, tablets, and smartphones.

3. User Experience (UX) Design: A well-designed website should be intuitive, easy to navigate, and visually appealing. Pay attention to factors such as site structure, navigation menus, and call-to-action buttons to enhance the user experience and encourage interaction.

4. Search Engine Optimization (SEO): Optimizing your website for search engines is crucial for increasing visibility and driving organic traffic. This involves optimizing on-page elements such as meta tags, headings, and keyword-rich content, as well as off-page factors like backlinks and social signals.

5. Conversion Rate Optimization (CRO): CRO focuses on optimizing your website to maximize the percentage of visitors who take desired actions, such as making a purchase or filling out a contact form. This may involve A/B testing,

optimizing landing pages, and streamlining the checkout process.

Actionable Tips for Website Optimization:

- Conduct a thorough website audit to identify areas for improvement.

- Optimize images and multimedia elements to reduce file sizes and improve load times.

- Implement responsive design principles to ensure a seamless experience across all devices.

- Use clear and intuitive navigation menus to help users find the information they're looking for.

- Optimize page titles, meta descriptions, and heading tags with relevant keywords to improve search engine visibility.

- Monitor website performance using tools like Google Analytics and make data-driven decisions to optimize your site further.

By implementing these website optimization strategies, you can create a faster, more user-friendly, and search engine-friendly website that drives engagement, conversions, and ultimately, business growth. In the next chapter, we'll delve into the intricacies of search engine optimization (SEO) and explore techniques for improving your site's visibility in search engine results pages (SERPs).

- **Search Engine Optimization (SEO)**

SEO is about understanding how search engines work and tailoring your website's content, structure, and performance to align with their algorithms. Search engines like Google, Bing, and Yahoo use complex algorithms to crawl, index, and rank billions of web pages based on various factors such as relevance, authority, and user experience. By optimizing your website for these factors, you can improve its chances of ranking higher in search results for relevant queries.

Key Components of SEO :

1. Keyword Research: Keywords are the foundation of SEO. Conducting keyword research involves identifying the terms and phrases that your target audience is searching for online and strategically incorporating them into your website's content. This helps search engines understand the relevance of your pages to specific queries and improves your chances of ranking for relevant search terms.

2. On-Page Optimization: On-page optimization involves optimizing various elements of your website's individual pages to improve their search engine visibility. This includes optimizing meta tags (such as title tags and meta descriptions), headings, and body content with relevant keywords, as well as optimizing images and multimedia elements for search.

3. Off-Page Optimization: Off-page optimization refers to activities conducted outside of your website to improve its authority and credibility in the eyes of search engines. This includes building high-quality backlinks from reputable websites, engaging in social media promotion, and earning positive reviews and mentions from customers and influencers.

4. Technical SEO: Technical SEO focuses on optimizing your website's technical infrastructure to improve its crawlability, indexability, and overall performance in search engines. This includes optimizing site speed, fixing broken links, implementing schema markup, and ensuring mobile-friendliness.

5. Content Quality and Relevance: Content is king in the world of SEO. Creating high-quality, relevant, and engaging content that satisfies the needs and interests of your target audience is essential for SEO success. This includes creating informative blog posts, product pages, guides, and other types of content that address common questions and pain points within your industry.

Actionable SEO Strategies:

- Conduct keyword research to identify relevant search terms and phrases.

- Optimize your website's on-page elements, including meta tags, headings, and body content, with target keywords.

- Create high-quality, informative content that provides value to your audience and encourages engagement and sharing.

- Build high-quality backlinks from reputable websites within your industry.

- Monitor your website's performance in search engine results pages (SERPs) using tools like Google Analytics and Google Search Console, and make adjustments as needed.

By implementing these SEO strategies, you can improve your website's visibility in search engine results, attract more organic traffic, and ultimately, achieve your business goals. In the next chapter, we'll explore the power of content marketing and how you can leverage it to enhance your SEO efforts and drive meaningful results for your business.

- **Content Marketing**

Content marketing is about storytelling. It's about creating compelling narratives that resonate with your audience, addressing their needs, interests, and pain points, and providing them with valuable insights, information, and entertainment. Unlike traditional advertising, which interrupts consumers' experiences with promotional messages, content marketing seeks to provide genuine value to its audience, earning their trust and loyalty in the process.

Key Components of Content Marketing :

1 - Identifying Your Audience: The first step in any successful content marketing strategy is understanding your target audience. Who are they? What are their interests, preferences, and pain points? By conducting thorough audience research, you can gain valuable insights into your audience's needs and tailor your content to address them effectively.

2 - Content Creation: Content creation is the heart of content marketing. This involves developing high-quality, relevant, and engaging content that resonates with your target audience. From blog posts and articles to videos, podcasts, infographics, and social

media posts, the possibilities for content creation are endless. The key is to create content that provides value to your audience and aligns with your brand's goals and messaging.

3 - Content Distribution: Creating great content is only half the battle. To maximize its impact, you need to ensure that it reaches your target audience. Content distribution involves promoting your content through various channels, including your website, social media platforms, email newsletters, and third-party publications. By strategically distributing your content across multiple channels, you can increase its visibility, reach, and engagement.

4 - Content Optimization: Content optimization involves ensuring that your content is easily discoverable by search engines and resonates with your target audience. This includes optimizing your content for relevant keywords, incorporating

multimedia elements to enhance engagement, and structuring your content in a way that is easy to read and navigate.

5 - Measuring Success: Like any marketing strategy, content marketing requires ongoing evaluation and optimization. By tracking key performance metrics such as website traffic, engagement, conversion rates, and social shares, you can assess the effectiveness of your content marketing efforts and make data-driven decisions to improve performance over time.

Actionable Content Marketing Strategies :

_ Conduct audience research to understand your target audience's needs, preferences, and pain points.

_ Develop a content strategy that aligns with your brand's goals and messaging.

_ Create high-quality, relevant, and engaging content that provides value to your audience.

_ Promote your content through various channels to increase its visibility and reach.

_ Monitor key performance metrics and adjust your content marketing strategy accordingly.

By implementing these content marketing strategies, you can attract and retain a loyal audience, enhance your brand's visibility and authority, and ultimately, drive meaningful results for your business. In the next chapter, we'll explore the power of social media marketing and how you can leverage it to amplify your content and engage with your audience on a deeper level.

- **Social Media Marketing**

Social media marketing is more than just posting content on Facebook, Instagram, Twitter, and other social platforms. It's about building relationships with your audience, fostering engagement, and creating meaningful connections that drive loyalty and advocacy for your brand. Whether you're a small startup or a global corporation, social media offers a level playing field for businesses of all sizes to connect with customers and showcase their unique value proposition.

Key Components of Social Media Marketing:

1 - Choosing the Right Platforms: With a multitude of social media platforms available, it's essential to choose the ones that align with your target audience and business objectives. Different platforms cater to different demographics and interests, so take the time to research and identify where your audience spends their time online.

2 - Building a Strong Presence: Once you've identified the right platforms, focus on building a strong presence by creating compelling profiles that

reflect your brand's personality and values. This includes optimizing your profiles with high-quality visuals, concise messaging, and relevant keywords to increase visibility and attract followers.

3 - Content Strategy: Content is the currency of social media. Develop a content strategy that resonates with your audience and aligns with your brand's goals and messaging. This may include a mix of curated content, original posts, videos, images, and interactive content formats such as polls, quizzes, and contests.

4 - Engagement and Community Management: Social media is all about conversation and interaction. Engage with your audience by responding to comments, messages, and mentions promptly, and actively participate in relevant discussions and conversations within your industry. Building a sense of community around your brand

can foster loyalty and advocacy among your followers.

5 - Paid Advertising: While organic reach on social media can be limited, paid advertising offers a powerful way to amplify your message and reach a wider audience. Platforms like Facebook Ads, Instagram Ads, and LinkedIn Ads allow you to target specific demographics, interests, and behaviors, ensuring that your content reaches the right people at the right time.

Actionable Social Media Marketing Strategies:

_ Research your target audience to understand their demographics, interests, and behavior on social media.

_ Develop a content strategy that aligns with your brand's goals and resonates with your audience.

_ Build a strong presence on the right social media platforms by optimizing your profiles and posting consistently.

_ Engage with your audience by responding to comments, messages, and mentions promptly and participating in relevant conversations.

_ Experiment with paid advertising to amplify your message and reach a wider audience.

By implementing these social media marketing strategies, you can build a loyal following, increase brand awareness and engagement, and drive meaningful results for your business. In the next chapter, we'll explore the essentials of email marketing and how you can leverage it to nurture leads, promote products or services, and build long-term relationships with your audience.

- **Email Marketing**

Email marketing involves sending targeted emails to prospects and customers with the goal of driving engagement, conversions, and customer loyalty. Unlike social media or other marketing channels, email marketing allows for personalized communication tailored to the recipient's preferences and behaviors. Whether it's a promotional offer, a newsletter, or a transactional email, email marketing enables businesses to deliver timely and relevant messages directly to their audience's inbox.

Key Components of Email Marketing:

1 - Building an Email List: The foundation of any successful email marketing campaign is a quality email list. Start by collecting email addresses from website visitors, social media followers, and customers through sign-up forms, pop-ups, and incentives such as discounts or freebies. It's essential to obtain permission from subscribers before

sending them marketing emails to comply with anti-spam regulations and build trust with your audience.

2 - Crafting Effective Email Campaigns: Once you have an email list, it's time to create compelling email campaigns that resonate with your audience and drive action. This may include promotional emails, newsletters, welcome emails, abandoned cart reminders, and more. Pay attention to factors such as subject lines, copywriting, design, and calls-to-action to ensure that your emails stand out and compel recipients to take the desired action.

3 - Personalization and Segmentation: Personalization is key to the success of email marketing. Use data such as demographics, purchase history, and browsing behavior to segment your email list and deliver targeted, relevant content to different audience segments. Personalized emails have higher open and click-through rates and are

more likely to drive conversions than generic, one-size-fits-all messages.

4 - Email Automation and Drip Campaigns: Email automation allows you to streamline your email marketing efforts by sending automated messages based on predefined triggers or actions. Drip campaigns, for example, are series of automated emails sent over time to nurture leads and guide them through the sales funnel. By automating repetitive tasks and delivering timely, personalized messages, you can increase efficiency and engagement while saving time and resources.

Actionable Email Marketing Strategies:

_ Build an email list by collecting email addresses from website visitors, social media followers, and customers.

_ Craft compelling email campaigns that resonate with your audience and drive action.

- Personalize your emails based on subscriber data to increase relevance and engagement.

- Implement email automation to streamline your email marketing efforts and deliver timely, personalized messages.

- Monitor key metrics such as open rates, click-through rates, and conversion rates to measure the effectiveness of your email campaigns and make data-driven decisions to optimize performance.

By implementing these email marketing strategies, you can effectively nurture leads, drive engagement, and build long-term relationships with your audience, ultimately driving meaningful results for your business. In the next chapter, we'll explore the essentials of paid advertising and how you can leverage platforms like Google Ads and Facebook Ads to reach your target audience and drive conversions.

- **Pay-Per-Click (PPC) Advertising**

PPC advertising is a digital advertising model in which advertisers pay a fee each time their ad is clicked. It allows businesses to bid on keywords relevant to their products or services and display ads prominently in search engine results pages (SERPs) or on other websites and platforms. Unlike traditional advertising models, where advertisers pay a fixed fee regardless of performance, PPC advertising offers a more cost-effective and measurable way to reach potential customers and drive traffic to your website.

Key Components of PPC Advertising:

1 - Keyword Research: Keyword research is the foundation of any successful PPC campaign. Start by identifying relevant keywords and phrases that

your target audience is likely to use when searching for products or services like yours. Use keyword research tools like Google Keyword Planner to discover new keywords, assess their search volume and competition, and determine their potential effectiveness for your campaign.

2 - Ad Creation: Once you've identified your target keywords, it's time to create compelling ads that resonate with your audience and compel them to click. Write concise, engaging ad copy that highlights the unique value proposition of your products or services and includes a clear call-to-action (CTA) to encourage users to take the desired action, whether it's making a purchase, signing up for a newsletter, or contacting your business.

3 - Ad Targeting: PPC advertising offers advanced targeting options that allow you to reach specific demographics, interests, and behaviors with your ads. Use targeting options such as location targeting,

device targeting, demographic targeting, and audience targeting to ensure that your ads are shown to the most relevant audience segments and maximize your campaign's effectiveness.

4 - Bid Management: In PPC advertising, advertisers bid on keywords and compete with other advertisers for ad placement. Bid management involves monitoring and adjusting your bids to ensure that you maintain a competitive position in the auction while maximizing your return on investment (ROI). Consider factors such as keyword performance, ad position, and budget constraints when adjusting your bids to optimize campaign performance.

Actionable PPC Advertising Strategies:

_ Conduct thorough keyword research to identify relevant keywords and phrases for your PPC campaigns.

_ Create compelling ad copy that highlights the unique value proposition of your products or services and includes a clear call-to-action.

_ Use advanced targeting options to reach specific demographics, interests, and behaviors with your ads.

_ Monitor and adjust your bids regularly to maintain a competitive position in the auction and maximize your ROI.

_ Track key metrics such as click-through rates, conversion rates, and cost per acquisition to measure the effectiveness of your PPC campaigns and make data-driven decisions to optimize performance.

By implementing these PPC advertising strategies, you can reach your target audience effectively, drive traffic to your website, and achieve your business objectives in a cost-effective and measurable way. In the next chapter, we'll explore the importance of analytics and measurement in digital marketing and how you can use data to inform your decision-making and drive continuous improvement in your marketing efforts.

• Influencer Marketing

Influencer marketing is based on the principle of social proof, which suggests that people are more likely to trust recommendations from individuals they know, admire, or perceive as experts in their field. Influencers, often with large and engaged followings on platforms like Instagram, YouTube, TikTok, and Twitter, have the ability to sway their audience's opinions and purchasing decisions through authentic and relatable content.

Key Components of Influencer Marketing:

1 - Identifying the Right Influencers: The success of your influencer marketing campaign hinges on partnering with the right influencers who resonate with your brand and target audience. Take the time to research and identify influencers whose values,

interests, and audience demographics align with your brand's goals and messaging. Look for influencers who have a genuine connection with their audience and a track record of producing high-quality, engaging content.

2 - Building Relationships: Once you've identified potential influencers, focus on building authentic and mutually beneficial relationships with them. Reach out to influencers with personalized pitches that highlight the value of partnering with your brand and demonstrate an understanding of their audience and content style. Cultivate relationships with influencers by engaging with their content, sharing their posts, and offering opportunities for collaboration beyond one-off campaigns.

3 - Campaign Planning and Execution: Collaborate with influencers to develop creative and engaging campaign concepts that align with your brand's objectives and resonate with their audience. Whether

it's sponsored posts, product reviews, giveaways, or takeover campaigns, work closely with influencers to ensure that the content is authentic, relevant, and compliant with advertising regulations. Provide influencers with clear guidelines and objectives for the campaign, but also allow them creative freedom to showcase your brand in their own unique voice.

4 - Measurement and Evaluation: As with any marketing initiative, it's essential to measure the success of your influencer marketing campaigns and evaluate their impact on your business goals. Track key metrics such as reach, engagement, website traffic, and conversions to gauge the effectiveness of your campaigns and make data-driven decisions for future collaborations. Collect feedback from influencers and analyze the performance of different campaign elements to identify areas for improvement and optimization.

Actionable Influencer Marketing Strategies:

_ Research and identify influencers whose values, interests, and audience demographics align with your brand.

_ Build authentic relationships with influencers through personalized outreach and engagement.

_ Collaborate with influencers to develop creative campaign concepts that resonate with their audience and achieve your brand's objectives.

_ Measure and evaluate the success of your influencer marketing campaigns using key metrics and feedback from influencers.

_ Continuously optimize and refine your influencer marketing strategy based on performance data and industry trends.

By implementing these influencer marketing strategies, you can tap into the power of social influence, reach new audiences, and build trust and credibility for your brand in the digital space. In the next chapter, we'll explore the importance of online public relations (PR) and how you can leverage it to manage your brand's reputation, build relationships with the media, and amplify your online presence.

- **Online Public Relations**

Online public relations encompasses a wide range of activities and tactics aimed at shaping public perception of your brand, managing crises, and amplifying positive messaging through digital channels. From crafting compelling press releases and pitching stories to journalists and bloggers to engaging with customers on social media and monitoring online conversations, online PR plays a vital role in building and maintaining a strong and reputable brand presence online.

Key Components of Online Public Relations:

1 - Media Relations: Media relations is a cornerstone of online PR, involving the cultivation of

relationships with journalists, bloggers, and influencers to secure positive coverage for your brand in online publications, blogs, and social media channels. This includes writing and distributing press releases, pitching story ideas, and responding to media inquiries promptly and professionally.

2 - Social Media Engagement: Social media has become a powerful platform for brands to engage with their audience, share news and updates, and manage their reputation in real-time. Online PR professionals monitor social media channels for mentions of their brand, respond to customer inquiries and feedback, and proactively engage with followers to build relationships and foster trust.

3 - Crisis Management: In the event of a crisis or negative publicity, online PR professionals play a crucial role in managing the situation and mitigating damage to the brand's reputation. This may involve issuing timely and transparent responses, addressing

concerns from customers and stakeholders, and proactively communicating updates and resolutions to the public.

4 - Online Reputation Management (ORM): ORM involves monitoring and managing online conversations and mentions of your brand to ensure that your online reputation remains positive and favorable. This includes monitoring online reviews, comments, and social media conversations, addressing negative feedback and complaints promptly, and generating positive content and testimonials to counteract any negative sentiment.

Actionable Online Public Relations Strategies:

_ Develop relationships with journalists, bloggers, and influencers in your industry to secure positive media coverage for your brand.

_ Monitor social media channels for mentions of your brand and engage with followers to build relationships and manage your online reputation.

_ Develop a crisis management plan to respond effectively to negative publicity or crises and protect your brand's reputation.

_ Implement online reputation management strategies to monitor and manage online conversations and ensure that your brand's reputation remains positive and favorable.

_ Continuously monitor and evaluate your online PR efforts using metrics such as media coverage, social media engagement, and sentiment analysis to gauge effectiveness and make data-driven decisions for future campaigns.

By implementing these online public relations strategies, you can effectively manage your brand's reputation, build relationships with key stakeholders, and enhance your brand's visibility and credibility in the digital space. In the final chapter, we'll recap key takeaways from this e-book and provide actionable tips for integrating these digital marketing strategies into your overall marketing strategy for maximum impact and success.

Chapter 3:

Developing a Digital Marketing Strategy

A digital marketing strategy is a comprehensive plan that outlines how your business will leverage digital channels, platforms, and tactics to achieve its marketing objectives. It encompasses everything from defining your target audience and value proposition to selecting the right mix of digital marketing channels and measuring the effectiveness of your campaigns. A well-defined digital marketing strategy provides a roadmap for your marketing efforts, ensuring that every action is aligned with your overall business goals and contributes to long-term success.

Key Components of a Digital Marketing Strategy:

1- Setting Clear Goals and Objectives : Start by defining clear and measurable objectives for your digital marketing efforts. Whether it's increasing brand awareness, driving website traffic, generating leads, or boosting sales, your objectives should be specific, achievable, and aligned with your overall business goals.

2- Identifying Your Target Audience : Understanding your target audience is crucial for crafting a successful digital marketing strategy. Conduct market research to identify your ideal customers' demographics, interests, preferences, and pain points. Use this information to create detailed buyer personas that guide your content creation, messaging, and targeting efforts.

3-Develop Your Value Proposition: Define your brand's unique value proposition – what sets you apart from the competition and why customers should choose your products or services over alternatives. Your value proposition should be clear, compelling, and consistently communicated across all digital marketing channels.

4- Choosing the Right Digital Marketing Channels : Based on your objectives, target audience, and budget, select the digital marketing channels and tactics that are most likely to reach and engage with your audience effectively. This may include search engine optimization (SEO), content marketing, social media marketing, email marketing, pay-per-click (PPC) advertising, influencer marketing, and more.

5- Create a Content Plan: Content lies at the heart of any successful digital marketing strategy. Develop a content plan that outlines the types of content you'll create, the topics you'll cover, and the channels you'll use to distribute it. Ensure that your content is valuable, relevant, and aligned with your audience's needs and interests.

6- Budgeting and Resource Allocation : Determine your digital marketing budget and allocate resources accordingly to ensure that you have the necessary funds and manpower to execute your strategy effectively. Consider factors such as advertising costs, content creation expenses, and staffing requirements when setting your budget.

7- Measure and Evaluate Performance: Implement tracking mechanisms and analytics tools to monitor the performance of your digital marketing campaigns and measure progress toward your objectives. Track key metrics such as website traffic, engagement, conversion rates, and return on investment (ROI) to assess the effectiveness of your strategy and make data-driven decisions for optimization and improvement.

By following these steps and crafting a well-defined digital marketing strategy, you can position your business for success in the digital landscape, reach your target audience effectively, and achieve your marketing objectives. In the conclusion of this e-book, we'll recap key takeaways and provide final thoughts on the importance of digital marketing in today's business environment.

Chapter 4:

Creating Compelling Content

In the digital realm, content is king. It serves as the foundation of your digital marketing efforts, attracting and engaging your audience, driving traffic to your website, and ultimately, converting leads into customers. In this chapter, we'll explore the power of content in digital marketing, delve into various types of content, discuss content creation strategies, and examine how to effectively distribute and promote your content for maximum impact.

The Power of Content in Digital Marketing

Content lies at the heart of digital marketing, serving as a powerful tool for building brand awareness, establishing authority and credibility, and nurturing relationships with your audience. Compelling content educates, entertains, and inspires, capturing the attention of your target audience and encouraging them to take action. Whether it's blog posts, videos, infographics, eBooks, or social media posts, well-crafted content has the potential to drive engagement, generate leads, and fuel business growth.

Types of Content

1. Blog Posts: Blogging is one of the most popular and effective forms of content marketing. Blog posts allow you to share valuable insights, industry news, tips, and how-to guides with your audience, positioning your brand as a thought leader in your niche.

2. Videos: Video content has exploded in popularity in recent years, offering a dynamic and engaging way to connect with your audience. From product demos and tutorials to behind-the-scenes footage and customer testimonials, videos allow you to tell your brand's story in a compelling and visual manner.

3. Infographics: Infographics combine visual elements such as charts, graphs, and illustrations with concise text to convey complex information in a visually appealing and easy-to-understand format. Infographics are highly shareable and can help drive traffic and engagement on social media platforms.

4. eBooks: eBooks are longer-form content pieces that provide in-depth information on a specific topic or subject matter. They're often used as lead magnets to capture email addresses and generate leads, offering valuable insights and expertise in exchange for contact information.

Content Creation Strategies

- Audience Research: Start by understanding your target audience's needs, preferences, and pain points. Conduct market research, surveys, and interviews to gather insights into what type of content resonates with your audience and addresses their challenges.

- Keyword Research: Conduct keyword research to identify relevant topics and keywords that your audience is searching for online. Use tools like Google Keyword Planner, SEMrush, or Ahrefs to discover high-volume and low-competition keywords to target in your content.

- Content Calendar: Develop a content calendar to plan and organize your content creation efforts. This ensures a consistent publishing schedule and helps you stay on track with your content goals.

- Content Optimization: Optimize your content for search engines by incorporating relevant keywords, meta tags, and headers. Use formatting techniques such as bullet points, numbered lists, and subheadings to improve readability and user experience.

Content Distribution and Promotion

- Social Media: Share your content across various social media platforms to reach a wider audience and encourage engagement. Use targeted advertising and sponsored posts to amplify your content's reach and visibility.

- Email Marketing: Promote your content to your email subscribers through newsletters, email campaigns, and automated drip sequences. Segment your email list based on interests and preferences to ensure that your content is relevant to each subscriber.

- Content Syndication: Syndicate your content on third-party websites, blogs, and publications to increase its exposure and reach new audiences. Look for opportunities to guest post or contribute articles to relevant industry publications.

- Influencer Outreach: Partner with influencers in your niche to promote your content to their engaged audience. Influencers can help amplify your message and lend credibility to your brand, driving traffic and engagement to your content.

By creating compelling content, you can capture the attention of your audience, drive engagement, and ultimately, achieve your digital marketing goals. In the next chapter, we'll explore the intricacies of website optimization and how you can maximize your site's potential to attract and retain visitors.

Chapter 5:

Maximizing Your Website's Potential

Your website serves as the digital storefront for your brand, making it essential to optimize its potential to attract, engage, and convert visitors into customers. In this chapter, we'll explore key strategies for maximizing your website's effectiveness, including designing a user-friendly interface, implementing SEO best practices, leveraging analytics for optimization, and focusing on conversion rate optimization (CRO) to drive meaningful results.

Designing a User-Friendly Website

A user-friendly website is essential for providing visitors with a positive experience and encouraging them to explore further. Here are some key principles to consider:

- Intuitive Navigation: Ensure that your website's navigation is clear, logical, and easy to use. Use descriptive labels and organize content hierarchically to help visitors find what they're looking for quickly and easily.

- Responsive Design: With an increasing number of users accessing the web from mobile devices, it's crucial to ensure that your website is mobile-friendly and responsive. This ensures a consistent and optimized experience across all devices and screen sizes.

- Page Load Speed: Optimize your website's load speed to minimize bounce rates and keep visitors engaged. Compress images, minimize HTTP requests, and leverage browser caching to improve performance.

- Clear Calls-to-Action (CTAs): Guide visitors toward desired actions with prominent and compelling CTAs strategically placed throughout your website. Whether it's signing up for a newsletter, making a purchase, or contacting your business, CTAs should be clear, concise, and visually appealing.

Implementing SEO Best Practices

Search engine optimization (SEO) is essential for ensuring that your website ranks well in search engine results pages (SERPs) and attracts organic traffic. Here are some key SEO best practices to implement:

- Keyword Optimization: Conduct keyword research to identify relevant terms and phrases related to your business. Optimize your website's content, meta tags, and headings with target keywords to improve visibility in search results.

- Quality Content: Create high-quality, relevant, and engaging content that addresses the needs and interests of your target audience. Regularly update your website with fresh content to keep visitors coming back and improve your search rankings.

- Technical Optimization: Ensure that your website is technically optimized for search engines by addressing issues such as site speed, mobile-friendliness, URL structure, and meta tags. Use tools like Google Search Console to identify and fix technical issues that may impact your site's performance.

Leveraging Analytics for Optimization

Analytics tools provide valuable insights into how visitors interact with your website, allowing you to identify areas for improvement and optimize your site for better performance. Here's how to leverage analytics effectively:

- Set Goals: Define specific goals and key performance indicators (KPIs) for your website, such as conversion rates, bounce rates, and average session duration.

- Track Metrics: Use analytics tools like Google Analytics to track and analyze key metrics related to your website's performance. Monitor traffic sources, user behavior, and engagement metrics to identify trends and areas for improvement.

- Make Data-Driven Decisions: Use data from analytics reports to inform your decision-making process and prioritize optimization efforts. Experiment with different strategies and tactics, and measure their impact on your website's performance over time.

Conversion Rate Optimization (CRO)

Conversion rate optimization (CRO) focuses on improving the percentage of website visitors who take a desired action, such as making a purchase, filling out a form, or subscribing to a newsletter. Here's how to optimize your website for conversions:

- Identify Conversion Points: Identify key conversion points on your website, such as product pages, landing pages, and checkout processes. Analyze user behavior and identify barriers to conversion.

- Optimize CTAs: Test different CTAs, button placements, colors, and messaging to determine which combinations drive the highest conversion rates.

- Simplify Forms: Streamline your forms and minimize the number of fields required to complete a conversion. Use progressive profiling to collect additional information over time.

- A/B Testing: Conduct A/B tests to compare different variations of your website elements and identify which versions perform best in terms of conversions.

By focusing on designing a user-friendly interface, implementing SEO best practices, leveraging analytics for optimization, and prioritizing conversion rate optimization (CRO), you can maximize your website's potential to attract, engage, and convert visitors into loyal customers. In the next chapter, we'll dive into the intricacies of search engine optimization (SEO) and explore advanced strategies for improving your website's visibility and ranking in search results.

Chapter 6:

Harnessing the Power of Social Media

Social media has transformed the way businesses connect with their audience, providing a platform for engagement, brand building, and driving conversions. In this chapter, we'll explore the strategies for effectively harnessing the power of social media, including choosing the right platforms, building a strong presence, engaging your audience with compelling content, and implementing social media advertising strategies to amplify your message.

- Choosing the Right Social Media Platforms :

Not all social media platforms are created equal, and it's essential to choose the ones that align with your business goals and target audience. Consider factors such as demographics, interests, and behavior to determine which platforms are most relevant for your brand.

Some popular social media platforms include:

Facebook: With over 2 billion monthly active users, Facebook offers a vast audience and diverse targeting options for businesses of all sizes.

Instagram: Known for its visual appeal, Instagram is ideal for businesses that rely heavily on visual content to showcase their products or services.

Twitter: Twitter is a real-time platform that's great for engaging with your audience, sharing news and updates, and participating in conversations related to your industry.

LinkedIn: LinkedIn is a professional networking platform that's well-suited for B2B businesses, offering opportunities to connect with industry professionals, share thought leadership content, and generate leads.

YouTube: As the second-largest search engine after Google, YouTube is a powerful platform for sharing video content and reaching a global audience.

- Building a Strong Social Media Presence

Once you've identified the right platforms for your business, focus on building a strong presence by:

Optimizing Your Profiles: Complete your social media profiles with accurate information, high-quality visuals, and relevant keywords to make a strong first impression.

Consistent Posting: Maintain a consistent posting schedule to keep your audience engaged and top of mind. Experiment with different types of content, such as text posts, images, videos, and stories, to keep your feed diverse and engaging.

Engaging with Your Audience: Actively engage with your audience by responding to comments, messages, and mentions promptly. Foster conversations, ask questions, and encourage user-generated content to build a sense of community around your brand.

-Engaging Your Audience with Compelling Content

Compelling content is the backbone of social media marketing. Here are some tips for creating content that resonates with your audience:

Know Your Audience: Understand your audience's interests, preferences, and pain points to create content that speaks to their needs and desires.

Tell Your Story: Use storytelling to humanize your brand and connect with your audience on a deeper level. Share behind-the-scenes content, customer testimonials, and employee spotlights to give followers a glimpse into your brand's personality and values.

Provide Value: Offer valuable and relevant content that educates, entertains, or inspires your audience. Whether it's how-to guides, tips and tricks, or industry insights, focus on providing content that enriches your audience's lives.

-Social Media Advertising Strategies

Social media advertising offers a powerful way to reach your target audience and amplify your message. Here are some strategies to consider:

Targeted Advertising: Use the targeting options available on social media platforms to reach specific demographics, interests, and behaviors with your ads. Narrow down your audience to ensure that your ads are shown to the most relevant users.

Compelling Ad Creative: Create visually appealing and attention-grabbing ad creative that stands out in users' feeds. Use high-quality images or videos, compelling copy, and clear calls-to-action to drive engagement and conversions.

A/B Testing: Experiment with different ad formats, targeting options, and messaging to determine which combinations drive the best results. Conduct A/B tests to compare different variations and optimize your campaigns for maximum effectiveness.

Chapter 7:

Email Marketing Essentials

Email marketing remains one of the most effective and cost-efficient ways to reach and engage with your audience. In this chapter, we'll explore the essential components of email marketing, including building an email list, crafting effective email campaigns, personalization and segmentation, and leveraging email automation and drip campaigns to nurture leads and drive conversions.

Building an Email List

Building an email list is the foundation of any successful email marketing strategy. Here's how to grow your email list:

- Website Opt-In Forms: Place opt-in forms on your website to capture email addresses from visitors. Offer incentives such as discounts, freebies, or exclusive content to encourage sign-ups.

- Social Media: Promote your email list on social media channels to reach a wider audience. Share links to sign-up forms and highlight the benefits of subscribing to your email list.

- Offline Events: Collect email addresses at offline events such as trade shows, conferences, or networking events. Use paper sign-up forms or QR codes to capture contact information.

Crafting Effective Email Campaigns

Once you've built your email list, it's time to craft compelling email campaigns that resonate with your audience. Here are some tips for crafting effective email campaigns:

- Clear Objectives: Define clear objectives for each email campaign, whether it's promoting a product launch, driving website traffic, or nurturing leads through the sales funnel.

- Compelling Subject Lines: Grab your subscribers' attention with compelling subject lines that entice them to open your emails. Use personalization, curiosity, urgency, or benefits-driven language to increase open rates.

- Engaging Content: Create engaging and relevant content that provides value to your subscribers. Whether it's informative articles, product updates, or special offers, focus on delivering content that resonates with your audience's needs and interests.

Personalization and Segmentation

Personalization and segmentation are key strategies for maximizing the effectiveness of your email marketing campaigns. Here's how to personalize and segment your email list:

- Personalization: Use personalization tokens to dynamically insert subscribers' names, locations, or other personalized information into your emails. Tailor your content and messaging to each subscriber's preferences and behaviors to increase engagement and relevance.

- Segmentation: Segment your email list based on demographics, interests, purchase history, or engagement level to deliver targeted and relevant content to different audience segments. Use segmentation criteria such as age, gender, location, or past interactions with your brand to tailor your emails for maximum impact.

Email Automation and Drip Campaigns

Email automation and drip campaigns allow you to streamline your email marketing efforts and deliver timely, personalized messages to your subscribers. Here's how to leverage email automation effectively:

- Welcome Emails: Set up automated welcome emails to greet new subscribers and introduce them to your brand. Use this opportunity to thank them for subscribing, provide information about your products or services, and encourage further engagement.

- Drip Campaigns: Create drip campaigns or email sequences to nurture leads and guide them through the sales funnel. Send a series of automated emails over time, delivering valuable content, addressing common objections, and encouraging conversions at each stage of the buyer's journey.

By implementing these email marketing essentials, you can effectively build and nurture relationships with your audience, drive engagement, and ultimately, drive conversions and revenue for your business. In the next chapter, we'll explore the fundamentals of paid advertising and how you can leverage platforms like Google Ads and Facebook Ads to reach your target audience and achieve your marketing goals.

Chapter 8:

Leveraging Paid Advertising

Paid advertising offers businesses the opportunity to reach their target audience quickly and effectively through various online platforms. In this chapter, we'll explore the fundamentals of paid advertising, including an introduction to PPC advertising, creating effective ad campaigns, popular ad platforms such as Google Ads and Facebook Ads, and tracking and measuring ROI to ensure optimal performance.

Introduction to PPC Advertising

PPC (Pay-Per-Click) advertising is a digital advertising model in which advertisers pay a fee each time their ad is clicked. It allows businesses to bid on keywords relevant to their products or services and display ads prominently in search engine results pages (SERPs) or on other websites. PPC advertising provides a cost-effective way to reach potential customers and drive targeted traffic to your website.

Creating Effective Ad Campaigns

Creating effective ad campaigns involves several key steps:

- Keyword Research: Conduct thorough keyword research to identify relevant keywords and phrases that your target audience is likely to use when searching for products or services like yours.

- Ad Copywriting: Write compelling ad copy that highlights the unique value proposition of your products or services and includes a clear call-to-action (CTA) to encourage users to click on your ads.

- Ad Targeting: Utilize advanced targeting options to ensure that your ads are shown to the most relevant audience segments. Target based on demographics, interests, behaviors, and more to maximize the effectiveness of your campaigns.

- Ad Design: Design visually appealing and attention-grabbing ad creatives that stand out in users' feeds and drive engagement. Test different ad formats, images, and messaging to determine which combinations perform best.

Ad Platforms: Google Ads, Facebook Ads, LinkedIn Ads, etc.

There are several popular ad platforms that businesses can leverage to reach their target audience:

- Google Ads: Formerly known as Google AdWords, Google Ads allows businesses to display ads in Google's search results and on the Google Display Network. With a wide range of targeting options and ad formats, Google Ads is suitable for businesses of all sizes and industries.

- Facebook Ads: Facebook Ads enables businesses to target users based on demographics, interests, behaviors, and more. With highly visual ad formats and advanced targeting capabilities, Facebook Ads is ideal for reaching a highly targeted audience on the world's largest social media platform.

- LinkedIn Ads: LinkedIn Ads is designed for B2B marketers looking to reach professionals and decision-makers on the world's largest professional networking platform. With targeting options such as job title, industry, company size, and more,

LinkedIn Ads allows businesses to reach a highly relevant audience.

Tracking and Measuring ROI

Tracking and measuring ROI is essential for evaluating the effectiveness of your paid advertising campaigns and optimizing performance. Here's how to track and measure ROI effectively:

- Conversion Tracking: Set up conversion tracking to monitor specific actions that users take after clicking on your ads, such as purchases, form submissions, or sign-ups.

- Analytics Integration: Integrate your ad platforms with analytics tools such as Google Analytics to track key metrics such as traffic, engagement, and conversions.

- ROI Calculation: Calculate ROI by comparing the revenue generated from your ad campaigns to the total cost of advertising. Consider factors such as ad spend, conversion rates, and customer lifetime value to determine the overall return on investment.

By leveraging paid advertising effectively, businesses can reach their target audience, drive traffic and conversions, and achieve their marketing goals in a cost-effective and measurable way. In the next chapter, we'll explore the importance of analytics and measurement in digital marketing and how businesses can use data to inform their decision-making and drive continuous improvement in their marketing efforts.

Chapter 9:

Measuring Success and Analytics

In the dynamic world of digital marketing, measuring success and analyzing data are essential for optimizing strategies, improving performance, and achieving business objectives. In this chapter, we'll delve into the key metrics to track in digital marketing, the use of tools like Google Analytics, and how to analyze data to inform strategic decision-making.

Key Metrics to Track in Digital Marketing

Tracking the right metrics is crucial for evaluating the effectiveness of your digital marketing efforts. Here are some key metrics to consider:

- Website Traffic: Monitor the number of visitors to your website, as well as traffic sources, referral sources, and user behavior patterns.

- Conversion Rate: Track the percentage of visitors who complete a desired action on your website, such as making a purchase, filling out a form, or signing up for a newsletter.

- Engagement Metrics: Measure engagement metrics such as bounce rate, time on site, pages per session, and social media engagement to assess the quality of user interactions with your content.

- ROI (Return on Investment): Calculate the return on investment for your digital marketing campaigns by comparing the revenue generated to the total cost of advertising and marketing efforts.

Using Google Analytics and Other Tools

Google Analytics is a powerful tool for tracking and analyzing website traffic, user behavior, and conversions. Here's how to leverage Google Analytics effectively:

- Set Up Goals and Funnels: Define specific goals and conversion actions on your website, such as completing a purchase or filling out a contact form. Set up funnels to track the steps users take to complete these goals.

- Track Campaign Performance: Use campaign tracking parameters to monitor the performance of your digital marketing campaigns. Tag your URLs with UTM parameters to track traffic and conversions from specific sources, mediums, and campaigns.

- Utilize Advanced Features: Explore advanced features of Google Analytics, such as custom reports, segments, and dashboards, to gain deeper insights into your website's performance and user behavior.

In addition to Google Analytics, there are other tools and platforms available for tracking and analyzing digital marketing data, such as:

- Social Media Analytics Tools: Platforms like Facebook Insights, Twitter Analytics, and LinkedIn Analytics provide insights into social media performance, audience demographics, and engagement metrics.

- Email Marketing Platforms: Email marketing platforms like Mailchimp, Constant Contact, and HubSpot offer analytics dashboards to track email open rates, click-through rates, and conversion metrics.

Analyzing Data to Inform Strategy

Analyzing data allows you to identify trends, patterns, and opportunities for optimization in your digital marketing strategy. Here's how to analyze data effectively:

- Identify Trends: Look for trends and patterns in your data to understand how different marketing channels, campaigns, and strategies are performing over time.

- Spot Opportunities: Identify areas for improvement and optimization based on data analysis. Look for opportunities to refine targeting, optimize ad creative, or adjust messaging to better resonate with your audience.

- Make Informed Decisions: Use data-driven insights to inform strategic decision-making and allocate resources effectively. Adjust your marketing strategy based on performance data and prioritize initiatives with the highest potential for impact.

By tracking key metrics, leveraging tools like Google Analytics, and analyzing data to inform strategy, businesses can gain valuable insights into their digital marketing efforts, optimize performance, and achieve their business objectives more effectively. In the final chapter, we'll recap key takeaways from this e-book and provide actionable tips for integrating these digital marketing strategies into your overall marketing strategy for maximum impact and success.

Conclusion

In the ever-evolving landscape of digital marketing, staying ahead requires a comprehensive understanding of the strategies, tools, and techniques that drive success. Throughout this e-book, we've explored the fundamental principles and advanced tactics of digital marketing, covering everything from website optimization and content creation to social media engagement, email marketing, paid advertising, and analytics.

At its core, digital marketing is about connecting with your audience in meaningful ways, providing value, and fostering long-term relationships that drive business growth. By leveraging the power of digital channels and platforms, businesses can reach their target audience more effectively, engage with them on a personal level, and drive conversions and revenue.

From building a user-friendly website and creating compelling content to leveraging social media, email marketing, and paid advertising, each chapter has provided actionable insights and strategies to help businesses maximize their online presence and achieve their marketing goals.

As we conclude this e-book, remember that digital marketing is not a one-size-fits-all approach. It requires continuous learning, experimentation, and adaptation to keep up with the evolving trends and technologies in the digital landscape. By staying informed, embracing innovation, and prioritizing the needs of your audience, you can position your business for success in the digital age.

Thank you for joining us on this journey through the world of digital marketing. We hope that the insights and strategies shared in this e-book will empower you to take your digital marketing efforts to new heights and achieve greater success in your business endeavors. Here's to your continued growth and success in the exciting and ever-changing world of digital marketing.